NATALIE THOMSON

WRAP

Try the tortilla hack with over 80 quick and easy recipes

hamlyn

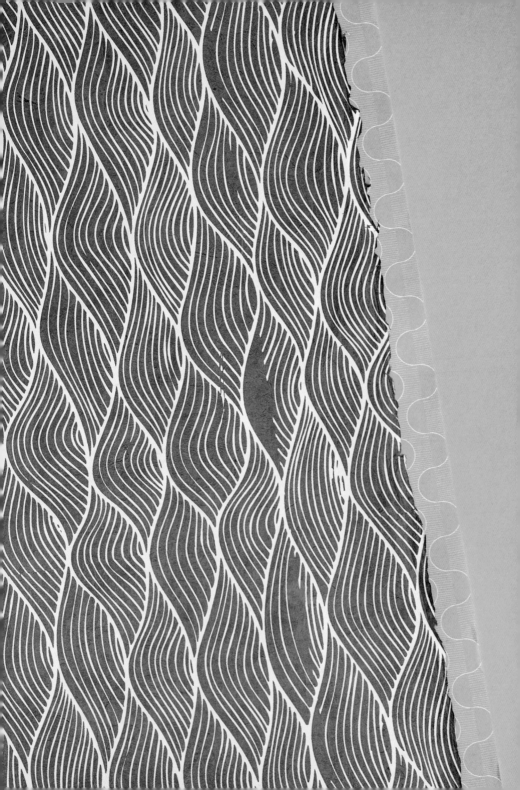

CONTENTS

INTRODUCTION

If you haven't yet tried the 'wrap hack', it's simply the smartest way to make a wrap and has taken social media and the world by storm. This ingenious method involves adding different ingredients to each quarter of a wrap and folding it up so that all the fillings are securely held in a neat package. So easy and fun to do, you wonder why we haven't always made wraps this way!

This game-changing technique makes quick and clever work of breakfasts, snacks, lunches and sweet treats, and is the ideal vehicle for leftovers. Not only will it lift you out of a sandwich rut, it will also get your creative juices flowing as you try out new flavour combinations with your family and friends.

Among the 80 recipes here are wrap-hack takes on some classic fillings, well-loved favourites and many exciting new combos, including plenty of vegetarian and vegan options. Plus there are suggestions for meat, fish or veggie alternatives, and warm or cold versions. The following symbols used throughout the book will help you spot what kind of recipe you are looking for at a glance.

 COLD   WARM   VEGGIE   VEGAN

WRAPS AND FILLINGS

You can use any type of wrap or soft tortilla – plain, wholemeal, seeded or flavoured. All the recipes are based on using a regular-sized wrap (19cm/7½in).

Gluten-free wraps also work well, but they may benefit from heating in a microwave for 10 seconds before use.

Wraps freeze really well, so keep a batch in the freezer for when you get peckish – it's best to place a piece of nonstick baking paper between each wrap and then stack in a freezer bag or freezerproof container so that they can be easily removed singly. Either defrost the wrap in a microwave for 20–30 seconds or leave in a cool, dry place until thoroughly defrosted. Then raid the refrigerator and fill and fold with whatever you fancy!

There is no limit to what ingredients you can combine in your wrap, although make sure they aren't too bulky or liquid, otherwise you will struggle to fold the wrap or prevent the filling from oozing out.

All raw meat or fish products and ready-made, shop-bought filling ingredients should be cooked according to the packet instructions before being used in a wrap. You will find instructions for cooking a few basic filling ingredients on pages 8–9.

If using leftovers in your wrap, ensure they are piping hot before serving.

Once you've folded your wrap (see pages 6–7), serve it as it is or toasted in a hot griddle pan, as instructed in the recipes. You could alternatively toast your wrap in a panini press, if you have one, following the manufacturer's instructions.

ASSEMBLING YOUR WRAP

1 Lay your wrap on a chopping board. Using a sharp knife, cut a slit from the centre downwards to the edge. In your mind, divide the wrap into quarters. Place a filling on each quarter.

2 Think of your wrap as an analogue clock face. To fold your wrap, take the first quarter, the 6–9 o'clock section, and fold it directly upwards over the next quarter, the 9–12 o'clock section.

3 Fold that section over the third quarter, the 12–3 o'clock section. Finally, fold again over the fourth section, the 3–6 o'clock section.

4 You will now have a neat triangular-shaped folded wrap that can either be enjoyed just as it is or toasted.

BASIC RECIPES

The following freshly cooked ingredients feature in some of the recipes in the book, so here are some simple guidelines on how to prepare them as a handy reference.

OMELETTE

Beat 2 eggs together in a bowl with a little salt and pepper.

Heat a small splash of oil in a frying pan over a low heat. Pour in the beaten eggs to cover the base of the pan and cook until firm on top with no visible runny egg.

Remove the pan from the heat, fold the omelette into quarters and use immediately.

Alternatively, use a ring mould in the pan to make a small, neat omelette. Turn once during cooking until golden on both sides.

SCRAMBLED EGGS

Beat 2 eggs together in a bowl with a little salt and pepper.

Heat a small splash of oil in a frying pan over a low heat. Pour in the beaten eggs and gradually stir with a spatula until you have large, fluffy pieces of lightly cooked egg.

Remove the pan from the heat and use the eggs immediately.

HARD-BOILED EGG

Place an egg in a small saucepan and just cover with cold water. Bring to the boil and cook for 6 minutes.

Remove the egg from the pan and place in a bowl of cold water until it is cool enough to shell.

SAUTÉED WHITE MUSHROOMS

Finely slice the mushrooms.

Heat a small splash of oil in a frying pan. Add the mushrooms and cook until softened and starting to turn golden. Season with salt and pepper.

PAN-FRIED HALLOUMI CHEESE

Cut the halloumi into slices about 3mm (⅛in) thick.

Heat a small splash of oil in a frying pan. Add the halloumi slices and cook over a high heat for 2–3 minutes. Flip and cook on the other side for another 2 minutes or until golden.

TOFU SCRAMBLE

Roughly chop up some firm tofu.

Heat a small splash of oil in a frying pan. Add the tofu with a little salt and pepper and use a wooden spoon to break down the tofu pieces to resemble scrambled eggs. Cook for 5–6 minutes until heated through.

MIXED ROASTED VEGETABLES

Preheat the oven to 200°C (400°F), Gas Mark 6.

Cut vegetables such as cored and deseeded peppers and trimmed courgettes and mushrooms into bite-sized pieces and spread out on a baking sheet.

Drizzle with a little oil, season with salt and pepper and roast for 20–25 minutes or until softened and golden.

BREAKFAST
& BRUNCH

SMOKED SALMON

1 regular wrap

100g (3½oz) smoked salmon

1 tablespoon cream cheese

1 teaspoon roughly chopped dill

pinch of freshly ground black pepper

1 teaspoon mashed capers

a few slices of red onion

Lay the wrap on a chopping board and cut a slit from the centre to the bottom edge.

In your mind, divide the wrap into quarters. Working clockwise, place the smoked salmon on the bottom left quarter, then spread the cream cheese over the next quarter and sprinkle with the dill and black pepper. Spread the capers over the third quarter and place the onion on the fourth.

Fold your wrap, then serve.

ALTERNATIVES

Mackerel: swap the smoked salmon for smoked mackerel.

Vegetarian: swap the smoked salmon for sun-dried tomatoes.

Meat: swap the smoked salmon for crispy streaky bacon and the dill for shredded lettuce.

COOKED BREAKFAST

1 regular wrap

1 hash brown, freshly cooked

1 freshly cooked omelette, made with 2 eggs

2 bacon rashers, freshly cooked

1 white mushroom, finely sliced

Lay the wrap on a chopping board and cut a slit from the centre to the bottom edge.

In your mind, divide the wrap into quarters. Working clockwise, place the hash brown on the bottom left quarter, the omelette on the next quarter, the bacon on the third and the mushrooms on the fourth.

Fold your wrap.

Place the wrap on a hot griddle pan and cook for 2 minutes. Flip and cook on the other side for a further 2 minutes until golden and toasted. Serve immediately.

CHORIZO & EGG

1 regular wrap

4–5 sun-dried tomatoes

small handful of rocket

5–6 slices of ready-to-eat chorizo

2 eggs, freshly scrambled

Lay the wrap on a chopping board and cut a slit from the centre to the bottom edge.

In your mind, divide the wrap into quarters. Working clockwise, place the sun-dried tomatoes on the bottom left quarter, the rocket on the next quarter, the chorizo on the third and the scrambled eggs on the fourth.

Fold your wrap, then serve.

Alternatively, place the wrap on a hot griddle pan and cook for 2 minutes. Flip and cook on the other side for a further 2 minutes until golden and toasted. Serve immediately.

TOFU SCRAMBLE

1 regular wrap

1 tablespoon vegan mayonnaise

½ avocado, sliced

small handful of spinach

1 large tomato, sliced

4 tablespoons freshly cooked tofu scramble

Lay the wrap on a chopping board and cut a slit from the centre to the bottom edge.

In your mind, divide the wrap into quarters. Working clockwise, spread the mayonnaise over the bottom left quarter and top with the avocado. Place the spinach on the next quarter, the tomato on the third and the tofu scramble on the fourth.

Fold your wrap.

Place the wrap on a hot griddle pan and cook for 2 minutes. Flip and cook on the other side for a further 2 minutes until golden and toasted. Serve immediately.

GRANOLA

1 regular wrap

2 tablespoons full-fat natural yogurt

2 tablespoons granola

1 tablespoon raspberry jam

2 strawberries, sliced

1 fig, sliced

Lay the wrap on a chopping board and cut a slit from the centre to the bottom edge.

In your mind, divide the wrap into quarters. Working clockwise, spread the yogurt over the bottom left quarter and sprinkle the granola on top, then spread the jam over the next quarter and place the strawberries on the third and the fig on the fourth.

Fold your wrap, then serve.

ALTERNATIVES

Warm: swap the yogurt for ricotta cheese and cook until golden and toasted.

Tropical: swap the raspberry jam for apricot jam, and the fruit for pineapple and kiwi.

Chocolate: swap the raspberry jam for chocolate spread.

SPICY EGGS

1 regular wrap

2 eggs, freshly scrambled

pinch of freshly ground black pepper

small handful of spinach

50g (1¾oz) vegetarian mature Cheddar cheese, grated

½ avocado, mashed

1 teaspoon hot sauce

Lay the wrap on a chopping board and cut a slit from the centre to the bottom edge.

In your mind, divide the wrap into quarters. Working clockwise, place the scrambled eggs on the bottom left quarter and sprinkle with the pepper. Place the spinach on the next quarter, the Cheddar on the third, then spread the avocado over the fourth and drizzle with the hot sauce.

Fold your wrap.

Place the wrap on a hot griddle pan and cook for 2 minutes. Flip and cook on the other side for a further 2 minutes until golden and toasted. Serve immediately.

BBLT

1 regular wrap

4–5 slices of Brie

2 bacon rashers, freshly cooked

small handful of rocket

1 tablespoon tomato jam or chutney

Lay the wrap on a chopping board and cut a slit from the centre to the bottom edge.

In your mind, divide the wrap into quarters. Working clockwise, place the Brie on the bottom left quarter, the bacon on the next quarter and the rocket on the third. Spread the jam or chutney over the fourth.

Fold your wrap.

Place the wrap on a hot griddle pan and cook for 2 minutes. Flip and cook on the other side for a further 2 minutes until golden and toasted. Serve immediately.

HALLOUMI & BEANS

1 regular wrap

3 slices of vegetarian halloumi cheese, freshly fried

100g (3½oz) drained canned mixed beans, heated and mashed

1 tablespoon aioli

1 roasted red pepper from a jar, sliced

small handful of spinach

Lay the wrap on a chopping board and cut a slit from the centre to the bottom edge.

In your mind, divide the wrap into quarters. Working clockwise, place the halloumi on the bottom left quarter and the beans on the next quarter, then spread the aioli over the third and top with the pepper and place the spinach on the fourth.

Fold your wrap, then serve.

SAUSAGE HASH

1 regular wrap

2–3 small potato rösti, freshly cooked

50g (1¾oz) Cheddar cheese, grated

1 freshly cooked omelette, made with 2 eggs

1 sausage, freshly cooked and sliced

Lay the wrap on a chopping board and cut a slit from the centre to the bottom edge.

In your mind, divide the wrap into quarters. Working clockwise, place the rösti on the bottom left quarter, the Cheddar on the next quarter, the omelette on the third and the sausages on the fourth.

Fold your wrap.

Place the wrap on a hot griddle pan and cook for 2 minutes. Flip and cook on the other side for a further 2 minutes until golden and toasted. Serve immediately.

REUBEN

1 regular wrap

2–3 slices of pastrami

50g (1¾oz) sauerkraut

50g (1¾oz) Gruyère cheese, grated

1 tablespoon mayonnaise

1 teaspoon creamed horseradish

Lay the wrap on a chopping board and cut a slit from the centre to the bottom edge.

In your mind, divide the wrap into quarters. Working clockwise, place the pastrami on the bottom left quarter, the sauerkraut on the next quarter, the Gruyère on the third and spread the mayonnaise and horseradish over the fourth.

Fold your wrap, then serve.

Alternatively, place the wrap on a hot griddle pan and cook for 2 minutes. Flip and cook on the other side for a further 2 minutes until the pastrami is piping hot and the wrap is golden and toasted. Serve immediately.

MARMITE & CHEESE

1 regular wrap

2 teaspoons Marmite

1 tablespoon cream cheese

50g (1¾oz) vegetarian Cheddar cheese, grated

1 spring onion, finely sliced

Lay the wrap on a chopping board and cut a slit from the centre to the bottom edge.

In your mind, divide the wrap into quarters. Working clockwise, spread the Marmite over the bottom left quarter and the cream cheese over the next quarter, then place the Cheddar on the third and the spring onion on the fourth.

Fold your wrap.

Place the wrap on a hot griddle pan and cook for 2 minutes. Flip and cook on the other side for a further 2 minutes until golden and toasted. Serve immediately.

CROQUE MONSIEUR

1 regular wrap

50g (1¾oz) Gruyère cheese, grated

3 tablespoons ready-prepared béchamel sauce

2–3 slices of ham

1 teaspoon Dijon mustard

Lay the wrap on a chopping board and cut a slit from the centre to the bottom edge.

In your mind, divide the wrap into quarters. Working clockwise, place the Gruyère on the bottom left quarter, spread the sauce over the next quarter, place the ham on the third and spread the mustard over the fourth.

Fold your wrap.

Place the wrap on a hot griddle pan and cook for 2 minutes. Flip and cook on the other side for a further 2 minutes until the ham is piping hot and the wrap is golden and toasted. Serve immediately.

QUICK LIGHT BITES

CHICKEN CAESAR

1 regular wrap

100g (3½oz) shredded cooked chicken

2 tablespoons Caesar dressing

2 tablespoons grated Parmesan cheese

small handful of shredded Little Gem lettuce or Romaine heart

1 hard-boiled egg, shelled and sliced, or 1 tomato, sliced

pinch of freshly ground black pepper

Lay the wrap on a chopping board and cut a slit from the centre to the bottom edge.

In your mind, divide the wrap into quarters. Working clockwise, place the chicken on the bottom left quarter, spread the Caesar dressing over the next quarter and sprinkle with the Parmesan. Place the lettuce on the third quarter and the egg or tomato on the fourth, sprinkled with the black pepper.

Fold your wrap, then serve.

SATAY CHICKEN

1 regular wrap

100g (3½oz) shredded cooked chicken

1 tablespoon smooth peanut butter

1 tablespoon natural yogurt

juice of ¼ lime

1 teaspoon sesame seeds

½ carrot, cut into matchsticks

a few slices of cucumber

small handful of spinach

Lay the wrap on a chopping board and cut a slit from the centre to the bottom edge.

In your mind, divide the wrap into quarters. Working clockwise, place the chicken on the bottom left quarter, then spread the peanut butter and yogurt over the next quarter, squeeze over the lime juice and sprinkle with the sesame seeds. Place the carrot and cucumber on the third quarter and the spinach on the fourth.

Fold your wrap, then serve.

ALTERNATIVES

Vegetarian: swap the chicken for griddled smoked tofu.

Vegan: swap the chicken for griddled smoked tofu and use vegan mayonnaise instead of yogurt.

Spicy: spread the first quarter with sweet chilli jam before adding the chicken and swap the sesame seeds for a sprinkle of dried chilli flakes.

SHREDDED DUCK

1 regular wrap

100g (3½oz) shredded cooked aromatic duck

small handful of shredded Little Gem lettuce or Romaine heart

1 spring onion, sliced

a few slices of cucumber

2 tablespoons hoisin sauce

Lay the wrap on a chopping board and cut a slit from the centre to the bottom edge.

In your mind, divide the wrap into quarters. Working clockwise, place the duck on the bottom left quarter, the lettuce on the next quarter and the spring onion and cucumber on the third, then spread the hoisin over the fourth.

Fold your wrap, then serve.

HAM & PINEAPPLE

1 regular wrap

100g (3½oz) shredded cooked ham hock or sliced ham

1 tablespoon pineapple jam

1 tablespoon soured cream

small handful of shredded white cabbage

½ carrot, cut into matchsticks

50g (1¾oz) Gruyère cheese, grated

Lay the wrap on a chopping board and cut a slit from the centre to the bottom edge.

In your mind, divide the wrap into quarters. Working clockwise, place the ham on the bottom left quarter and spread the pineapple jam over the next quarter. Spread the third quarter with the the soured cream and top with the cabbage and carrot, then place the Gruyère on the fourth.

Fold your wrap, then serve.

CLUB SANDWICH

1 regular wrap
_____

100g (3½oz) shredded
cooked chicken
_____

2 bacon rashers,
freshly cooked
_____

4 tablespoons
egg mayonnaise
_____

small handful of mixed
salad leaves

Lay the wrap on a chopping board and cut a slit from the centre to the bottom edge.

In your mind, divide the wrap into quarters. Working clockwise, place the chicken on the bottom left quarter, the bacon on the next quarter, the egg mayonnaise on the third and the salad leaves on the fourth.

Fold your wrap, then serve.

Alternatively, place the wrap on a hot griddle pan and cook for 2 minutes. Flip and cook on the other side for a further 2 minutes until the fillings are piping hot and the wrap is golden and toasted. Serve immediately.

PROSCIUTTO & NECTARINE

1 regular wrap

2 slices of prosciutto

small handful of rocket

½ nectarine, sliced

1 teaspoon honey

50g (1¾oz) Gorgonzola cheese, crumbled

Lay the wrap on a chopping board and cut a slit from the centre to the bottom edge.

In your mind, divide the wrap into quarters. Working clockwise, place the prosciutto on the bottom left quarter, the rocket on the next quarter, the nectarine on the third drizzled with the honey, then the Gorgonzola on the fourth.

Fold your wrap, then serve.

ALTERNATIVES

Extra Cheesy: swap the prosciutto for grated Gruyère cheese.

Vegan: swap the prosciutto for grated vegan cheese, the honey for agave nectar and swap the Gorgonzola for vegan mayonnaise.

Mediterranean: swap the nectarine for sliced tomatoes and the Gorgonzola for mozzarella.

BANH MI

1 regular wrap

1 tablespoon mayonnaise

1 teaspoon sriracha

½ carrot, cut into matchsticks

a chunk of cucumber, cut into matchsticks

2 tablespoons smooth pâté

3–4 slices of cooked turkey, ham or chicken

Lay the wrap on a chopping board and cut a slit from the centre to the bottom edge.

In your mind, divide the wrap into quarters. Working clockwise, spread the mayonnaise and sriracha over the bottom left quarter, place the carrot and cucumber on the next quarter, spread the pâté over the third and place the meat on the fourth.

Fold your wrap, then serve.

PULLED PORK

1 regular wrap

100g (3½oz) ready-prepared pulled pork, freshly cooked and shredded

2–3 tablespoons coleslaw

a few slices of red onion

5–6 coriander leaves

2 tablespoons barbecue sauce

Lay the wrap on a chopping board and cut a slit from the centre to the bottom edge.

In your mind, divide the wrap into quarters. Working clockwise, place the pork on the bottom left quarter, the coleslaw on the next quarter and the onion and coriander on the third, then spread the barbecue sauce over the fourth.

Fold your wrap.

Place the wrap on a hot griddle pan and cook for 2 minutes. Flip and cook on the other side for a further 2 minutes until golden and toasted. Serve immediately.

SPICY FISH STRIPS

1 regular wrap

3 fish goujons, freshly cooked

1 tablespoon aioli

1 red chilli, sliced

½ avocado, mashed

1 teaspoon sliced green jalapeños from a jar

a few slices of cucumber

Lay the wrap on a chopping board and cut a slit from the centre to the bottom edge.

In your mind, divide the wrap into quarters. Working clockwise, place the fish goujons on the bottom left quarter, then spread the aioli over the next quarter and top with the fresh chilli. Place the avocado on the third quarter and top with the jalapeños, then place the cucumber on the fourth.

Fold your wrap.

Place the wrap on a hot griddle pan and cook for 2 minutes. Flip and cook on the other side for a further 2 minutes until golden and toasted. Serve immediately.

SMOKED MACKEREL & BEETROOT

1 regular wrap

1 tablespoon mayonnaise

1 smoked mackerel fillet, skinned and flaked into bite-sized pieces

pinch of freshly ground black pepper

small handful of watercress

2 tablespoons beetroot hummus

1 teaspoon creamed horseradish

Lay the wrap on a chopping board and cut a slit from the centre to the bottom edge.

In a bowl, toss together the mayonnaise and smoked mackerel.

In your mind, divide the wrap into quarters. Working clockwise, place the mackerel on the bottom left quarter sprinkled with the pepper, then place the watercress on the next quarter. Spread the beetroot hummus over the third and the horseradish over the fourth.

Fold your wrap, then serve.

ALTERNATIVES

Vegetarian: swap the mackerel for chargrilled artichoke hearts or sun-dried tomatoes from a jar.

Vegan: swap the mackerel for roasted beetroot slices and use vegan mayonnaise.

Meat: swap the mackerel for sliced roast beef.

TUNA MELT

1 regular wrap

a chunk of cucumber, finely chopped

a few slices of red onion

2 teaspoons mayonnaise

100g (3½oz) drained canned tuna, flaked

2 slices of mature Cheddar cheese

Lay the wrap on a chopping board and cut a slit from the centre to the bottom edge.

In your mind, divide the wrap into quarters. Working clockwise, place the cucumber on the bottom left quarter and the onion on the next quarter. Spread the mayonnaise over the third quarter and top with the tuna, then place the Cheddar on the fourth.

Fold your wrap.

Place the wrap on a hot griddle pan and cook for 2 minutes. Flip and cook on the other side for a further 2 minutes until golden and toasted. Serve immediately.

PRAWN COCKTAIL

1 regular wrap

1 tablespoon lemon mayonnaise

100g (3½oz) cooked peeled prawns

small handful of shredded Iceberg lettuce

a few slices of cucumber

6-7 prawn crackers, broken up

Lay the wrap on a chopping board and cut a slit from the centre to the bottom edge.

In your mind, divide the wrap into quarters. Working clockwise, spread the mayonnaise over the bottom left quarter and top with the prawns, then place the lettuce on the next quarter, the cucumber on the third and the prawn crackers on the fourth.

Fold your wrap, then serve.

FENNEL SALAMI

1 regular wrap

5–6 slices of fennel salami

50g (1¾oz) ricotta cheese

1 tablespoon grated Parmesan

2 tablespoons drained chargrilled, marinated artichoke hearts from a jar

small handful of rocket

Lay the wrap on a chopping board and cut a slit from the centre to the bottom edge.

In your mind, divide the wrap into quarters. Working clockwise, place the salami on the bottom left quarter, the ricotta and Parmesan on the next quarter, the artichoke on the third and the rocket on the fourth.

Fold your wrap, then serve.

KOREAN BLUE CHEESE

1 regular wrap

30g (1oz) vegetarian blue cheese, crumbled

30g (1oz) vegetarian Cheddar cheese, grated

a few slices of red onion

50g (1¾oz) kimchi

1 tablespoon gochujang (Korean red chilli paste)

Lay the wrap on a chopping board and cut a slit from the centre to the bottom edge.

In your mind, divide the wrap into quarters. Working clockwise, place the cheeses on the bottom left quarter, the onion on the next quarter and the kimchi on the third, then spread the gochujang over the fourth.

Fold your wrap.

Place the wrap on a hot griddle pan and cook for 2 minutes. Flip and cook on the other side for a further 2 minutes until golden and toasted. Serve immediately.

ALTERNATIVES

Vegan: swap the two cheeses for vegan cream cheese and sliced spring onions.

Meat: swap the blue cheese for shredded chicken or pulled pork and toast until the fillings are piping hot.

Cold: swap the gochujang for sweet chilli sauce and enjoy the wrap without toasting.

BRIE, CRANBERRY & APPLE

1 regular wrap

½ apple, cored and sliced

small handful of spinach

4–5 slices of vegetarian Brie

1 tablespoon cranberry sauce

Lay the wrap on a chopping board and cut a slit from the centre to the bottom edge.

In your mind, divide the wrap into quarters. Working clockwise, place the apple on the bottom left quarter, the spinach on the next quarter, the Brie on the third and then spread the cranberry sauce over the fourth.

Fold your wrap, then serve.

Alternatively, place the wrap on a hot griddle pan and cook for 2 minutes. Flip and cook on the other side for a further 2 minutes until golden and toasted. Serve immediately.

CHILLI JAM
& CHEESE

1 regular wrap

1 tablespoon chilli jam

50g (1¾oz) mature Cheddar cheese, grated

3 slices of halloumi cheese, freshly fried

2–3 slices of Gorgonzola cheese

Lay the wrap on a chopping board and cut a slit from the centre to the bottom edge.

In your mind, divide the wrap into quarters. Working clockwise, spread the chilli jam over the bottom left quarter, then place the Cheddar on the next quarter, the halloumi on the third and the Gorgonzola on the fourth.

Fold your wrap.

Place the wrap on a hot griddle pan and cook for 2 minutes. Flip and cook on the other side for a further 2 minutes until golden and toasted. Serve immediately.

BABA GHANOUSH

1 regular wrap

2 tablespoons baba ghanoush

1 tablespoon tahini

1 tablespoon vegan mayonnaise or aioli

small handful of shredded kale

1–2 slices of tomato

a few slices of red onion

1 radish, sliced

Lay the wrap on a chopping board and cut a slit from the centre to the bottom edge.

In your mind, divide the wrap into quarters. Working clockwise, spread the baba ghanoush over the bottom left quarter and the tahini and mayonnaise or aioli over the next quarter, then place the kale on the third and the tomato, onion and radish on the fourth.

Fold your wrap, then serve.

PICKLED BEETROOT & CHEDDAR

1 regular wrap

2 pickled beetroots, sliced

1 tablespoon mayonnaise

1 teaspoon sliced green jalapeños from a jar

50g (1¾oz) vegetarian Cheddar cheese, grated

1 tablespoon vegetarian basil pesto

Lay the wrap on a chopping board and cut a slit from the centre to the bottom edge.

In your mind, divide the wrap into quarters. Working clockwise, place the beetroot on the bottom left quarter, spread the mayonnaise over the next quarter and top with the jalapeños, place the Cheddar on the third and spread the pesto over the fourth.

Fold your wrap.

Place the wrap on a hot griddle pan and cook for 2 minutes. Flip and cook on the other side for a further 2 minutes until golden and toasted. Serve immediately.

ALTERNATIVES

Meat: swap the beetroot for spicy salami.

Mexican: swap the beetroot for quick-pickled red onions and the pesto for yogurt and chipotle paste.

Vegan: swap the cheese for griddled smoked tofu or tempeh and use vegan mayonnaise and pesto.

STILTON & APPLE

1 regular wrap

50g (1¾oz) vegetarian Stilton cheese, sliced or crumbled

1 tablespoon apple sauce

2 tablespoons roasted, salted pecans, roughly chopped

small handful of rocket

Lay the wrap on a chopping board and cut a slit from the centre to the bottom edge.

In your mind, divide the wrap into quarters. Working clockwise, place the Stilton on the bottom left quarter, spread the apple sauce over the next quarter and place the pecans on the third and the rocket on the fourth.

Fold your wrap, then serve.

GOATS' CHEESE
& COURGETTE

1 regular wrap

50g (1¾oz) soft goats' cheese

¼ courgette, peeled with a vegetable peeler into ribbons

1 tablespoon vegetarian basil pesto

small handful of spinach

Lay the wrap on a chopping board and cut a slit from the centre to the bottom edge.

In your mind, divide the wrap into quarters. Working clockwise, spread the goats' cheese over the bottom left quarter, place the courgette on the next quarter, spread the pesto over the third and place the spinach on the fourth.

Fold your wrap, then serve.

GREEK

1 regular wrap

5–6 slices of roasted aubergine from a jar

1 tablespoon tzatziki

30g (1oz) vegetarian feta cheese, crumbled

a few slices of red onion

3–4 pitted Kalamata olives, roughly chopped

6–7 mint leaves

1 tomato, sliced

Lay the wrap on a chopping board and cut a slit from the centre to the bottom edge.

In your mind, divide the wrap into quarters. Working clockwise, place the aubergine on the bottom left quarter, then spread the tzatziki over the next quarter and top with the feta. Place the onion and olives on the third quarter and the mint and tomato on the fourth.

Fold your wrap, then serve.

ANTIPASTI

1 regular wrap

2 tablespoons drained chargrilled, marinated artichoke hearts from a jar

5–6 sun-dried tomatoes

1 tablespoon vegetarian basil pesto

½ mozzarella cheese ball, about 60g (2¼oz), shredded

Lay the wrap on a chopping board and cut a slit from the centre to the bottom edge.

In your mind, divide the wrap into quarters. Working clockwise, place the artichokes on the bottom left quarter, the sun-dried tomatoes on the next quarter, spread the pesto over the third and place the mozzarella on the fourth.

Fold your wrap.

Place the wrap on a hot griddle pan and cook for 2 minutes. Flip and cook on the other side for a further 2 minutes until golden and toasted. Serve immediately.

HUNGER
FIXES

SPICY FRIED CHICKEN

1 regular wrap
___

2 chicken goujons,
freshly cooked
___

small handful of
shredded Iceberg lettuce
___

50g (1¾oz) mature
Cheddar cheese, grated
___

1 tablespoon mayonnaise
___

1 teaspoon hot sauce

Lay the wrap on a chopping board and cut a slit from the centre to the bottom edge.

In your mind, divide the wrap into quarters. Working clockwise, place the chicken goujons on the bottom left quarter, the lettuce on the next quarter and the Cheddar on the third, then spread the mayonnaise and hot sauce over the fourth.

Fold your wrap.

Place the wrap on a hot griddle pan and cook for 2 minutes. Flip and cook on the other side for a further 2 minutes until golden and toasted. Serve immediately.

BURRITO

1 regular wrap

100g (3½oz) ready-prepared chilli con carne, heated

small handful of shredded Iceberg lettuce

2–3 slices of tomato

50g (1¾oz) mature Cheddar cheese, grated

2 tablespoons soured cream

5–6 tortilla chips, crumbled

Lay the wrap on a chopping board and cut a slit from the centre to the bottom edge.

In your mind, divide the wrap into quarters. Working clockwise, place the chilli on the bottom left quarter, the lettuce and tomato on the next quarter and the Cheddar on the third, then spread the soured cream over the fourth and top with the tortilla chips.

Fold your wrap.

Place the wrap on a hot griddle pan and cook for 2 minutes. Flip and cook on the other side for a further 2 minutes until the fillings are piping hot and the wrap is golden and toasted. Serve immediately.

VEGGIE BURRITO

1 regular wrap

100g (3½oz) canned vegetarian refried beans, heated

½ avocado, mashed

1 teaspoon hot sauce

7–8 tortilla chips, crumbled

small handful of shredded Iceberg lettuce

Lay the wrap on a chopping board and cut a slit from the centre to the bottom edge.

In your mind, divide the wrap into quarters. Working clockwise, place the refried beans on the bottom left quarter and the avocado on the next quarter, drizzled with the hot sauce. Place the tortilla chips on the third quarter and the lettuce on the fourth.

Fold your wrap, then serve.

PEPPERONI PIZZA

1 regular wrap

a few slices of red onion

1 tablespoon sweetcorn kernels

3–4 slices of pepperoni

½ mozzarella cheese ball, about 60g (2¼oz), shredded

2 tablespoons tomato sauce

½ teaspoon dried oregano

4 basil leaves

Lay the wrap on a chopping board and cut a slit from the centre to the bottom edge.

In your mind, divide the wrap into quarters. Working clockwise, place the onion and sweetcorn on the bottom left quarter and the pepperoni on the next quarter. Place the mozzarella on the third and the tomato sauce on the fourth, sprinkled with the herbs.

Fold the wrap.

Place the wrap on a hot griddle pan and cook for 2 minutes. Flip and cook on the other side for a further 2 minutes until the fillings are piping hot and the wrap is golden and toasted. Serve immediately.

PULLED JACKFRUIT

1 regular wrap

100g (3½oz) ready-prepared barbecue pulled jackfruit, freshly cooked

1 large roasted red pepper from a jar, sliced

a few slices of Cheddar-style vegan cheese

½ avocado, mashed

Lay the wrap on a chopping board and cut a slit from the centre to the bottom edge.

In your mind, divide the wrap into quarters. Working clockwise, place the barbecue jackfruit on the bottom left quarter, the sliced pepper on the next quarter, the cheese slices on the third and the avocado on the fourth.

Fold your wrap.

Place the wrap on a hot griddle pan and cook for 2 minutes. Flip and cook on the other side for a further 2 minutes until golden and toasted. Serve immediately.

MEATBALL SUB

1 regular wrap

2 tablespoons tomato sauce

4–5 meatballs, freshly cooked and broken up

½ mozzarella cheese ball, about 60g (2½oz), shredded

small handful of spinach

1 teaspoon crispy onions

Lay the wrap on the chopping board and cut a slit from the centre to the bottom edge.

In your mind, divide the wrap into quarters. Working clockwise, spread the tomato sauce over the bottom left quarter, then place the meatballs on the next quarter, the mozzarella on the third and the spinach and crispy onions on the fourth.

Fold your wrap.

Place the wrap on a hot griddle pan and cook for 2 minutes. Flip and cook on the other side for a further 2 minutes until golden and toasted. Serve immediately.

ALTERNATIVES

Vegetarian meatball: swap the meatballs for vegetarian meatballs.

Falafel: swap the meatballs for falafel, the tomato sauce for hummus and the mozzarella for garlic yogurt, and serve cold.

Extra Meaty: swap the crispy onions for crispy fried bacon.

ONION BHAJI

1 regular wrap

1 large onion bhaji, heated and broken up

2 tablespoons raita

2 tablespoons mango chutney

small handful of broken-up poppadum

Lay the wrap on a chopping board and cut a slit from the centre to the bottom edge.

In your mind, divide the wrap into quarters. Working clockwise, place the onion bhaji on the bottom left quarter and spread the raita over the next quarter and the mango chutney over the third, then place the poppadum on the fourth.

Fold your wrap.

Place the wrap on a hot griddle pan and cook for 2 minutes. Flip and cook on the other side for a further 2 minutes until golden and toasted. Serve immediately.

ROASTED VEGETABLE 🔥❄️✓

1 regular wrap

100g (3½oz) ready-prepared mixed roasted vegetables, such as peppers, courgettes and mushrooms

small handful of shredded kale

1 tablespoon aioli

pinch of freshly ground black pepper

50g (1¾oz) vegetarian feta cheese, crumbled

Lay the wrap on a chopping board and cut a slit from the centre to the bottom edge.

In your mind, divide the wrap into quarters. Working clockwise, place the vegetables on the bottom left quarter and the kale on the next quarter. Spread the aioli over the third and sprinkle with the black pepper, then place the feta on the fourth.

Fold your wrap, then serve.

Alternatively, place the wrap on a hot griddle pan and cook for 2 minutes. Flip and cook on the other side for a further 2 minutes until golden and toasted. Serve immediately.

CHEESE & BACON BURGER

1 regular wrap

1 burger, freshly cooked

1 cheese slice

2 bacon rashers, freshly cooked and chopped

1 teaspoon burger sauce

1 teaspoon mustard

small handful of shredded Iceberg lettuce

1 slice of tomato

a few slices of red onion

Lay the wrap on the chopping board and cut a slit from the centre to the bottom edge.

In your mind, divide the wrap into quarters. Working clockwise, place the burger on the bottom left quarter, then place the cheese on the next quarter and top with the bacon. Spread the burger sauce and mustard over the third quarter and place the lettuce, tomato and onion on the fourth.

Fold your wrap.

Place the wrap on a hot griddle pan and cook for 2 minutes. Flip and cook on the other side for a further 2 minutes until golden and toasted. Serve immediately.

ALTERNATIVES

Vegetarian: swap the burger for a vegetarian burger and the bacon for sautéed white mushrooms.

Extra Cheesy: swap the bacon for extra cheese slices.

Vegan: swap the burger for a vegan burger, the bacon for sliced avocado and use vegan cheese.

VEGAN BURGER

1 regular wrap

1 vegan burger, freshly cooked

a few slices of Cheddar-style vegan cheese

1 teaspoon tomato ketchup

1 teaspoon mustard

small handful of salad leaves

Lay the wrap on a chopping board and cut a slit from the centre to the bottom edge.

In your mind, divide the wrap into quarters. Working clockwise, place the burger on the bottom left quarter and the cheese on the next quarter, then spread the ketchup and mustard over the third and place the salad leaves on the fourth.

Fold your wrap.

Place the wrap on a hot griddle pan and cook for 2 minutes. Flip and cook on the other side for a further 2 minutes until golden and toasted. Serve immediately.

ALTERNATIVES

Chilli: swap the ketchup and mustard for bean chilli, heated before putting in the wrap.

Mexican: swap the cheese for guacamole and the ketchup and mustard for tortilla chips.

Pineapple: swap the cheese for a charred pineapple slice and the ketchup and mustard for barbecue sauce.

CHICKEN &
BLUE CHEESE

1 regular wrap

2 chicken goujons, freshly cooked

small handful of mixed salad leaves

1 tablespoon natural yogurt

2 tablespoons crumbled blue cheese

1 teaspoon hot sauce

Lay the wrap on a chopping board and cut a slit from the centre to the bottom edge.

In your mind, divide the wrap into quarters. Working clockwise, place the chicken goujons on the bottom left quarter and the salad on the next quarter. Spread the yogurt over the third quarter and top with the blue cheese, then spread the hot sauce over the fourth.

Fold your wrap, then serve.

Alternatively, place the wrap on a hot griddle pan and cook for 2 minutes. Flip and cook on the other side for a further 2 minutes until golden and toasted. Serve immediately.

LEFTOVER CHILLI

1 regular wrap

½ avocado, mashed

5–6 coriander leaves

2 tablespoons sweetcorn kernels

1 tablespoon sliced green jalapeños from a jar

100g (3½oz) ready-prepared chilli con carne, heated

50g (1¾oz) Cheddar cheese, grated

Lay the wrap on a chopping board and cut a slit from the centre to the bottom edge.

In your mind, divide the wrap into quarters. Working clockwise, place the avocado and coriander on the bottom left quarter, the sweetcorn and jalapeños on the next quarter, the chilli on the third and the Cheddar on the fourth.

Fold your wrap.

Place the wrap on a hot griddle pan and cook for 2 minutes. Flip and cook on the other side for a further 2 minutes until the fillings are piping hot and the wrap is golden and toasted. Serve immediately.

PO' BOY

1 regular wrap

1 tablespoon mayonnaise

small handful of shredded celeriac or white cabbage

6–7 breaded prawns, freshly cooked

1 teaspoon hot sauce

1 gherkin, sliced

small handful of shredded Iceberg lettuce

2 slices of tomato

Lay the wrap on a chopping board and cut a slit from the centre to the bottom edge.

In a bowl, toss together the mayonnaise and celeriac or cabbage.

In your mind, divide the wrap into quarters. Working clockwise, place the prawns on the bottom left quarter and the celeriac or cabbage on the next quarter, topped with the hot sauce. Place the gherkins on the third quarter and the lettuce and tomato on the fourth.

Fold your wrap, then serve.

ALTERNATIVES

Vegetarian: swap the prawns for roasted mushrooms.

BLT: swap the prawns for smoked streaky bacon.

Vegan: swap the prawns for falafel and use vegan mayonnaise.

SAUSAGE & CARAMELIZED ONION

1 regular wrap

1 sausage, freshly cooked and sliced

2 tablespoons caramelized onion chutney

2 tablespoons mayonnaise

1 teaspoon wholegrain mustard

small handful of spinach

Lay the wrap on a chopping board and cut a slit from the centre to the bottom edge.

In your mind, divide the wrap into quarters. Working clockwise, place the sausage on the bottom left quarter, spread the chutney over the next quarter and the mayonnaise and mustard over the third and then place the spinach on the fourth.

Fold your wrap.

Place the wrap on a hot griddle pan and cook for 2 minutes. Flip and cook on the other side for a further 2 minutes until golden and toasted. Serve immediately.

GYROS

1 regular wrap

100g (3½oz) shredded cooked chicken

pinch of dried oregano

2 tablespoons tzatziki

1 slice of tomato

small handful of shredded Iceberg lettuce

a few slices of red onion

50g (1¾oz) French fries, freshly cooked

Lay the wrap on a chopping board and cut a slit from the centre to the bottom edge.

In your mind, divide the wrap into quarters. Working clockwise, place the chicken on the bottom left quarter and sprinkle with the oregano. Spread the tzatziki over the next quarter, the tomato, lettuce and onion on the third and the chips on the fourth.

Fold your wrap.

Place the wrap on a hot griddle pan and cook for 2 minutes. Flip and cook on the other side for a further 2 minutes until the chicken is piping hot and the wrap is golden and toasted. Serve immediately.

PHILLY CHEESE STEAK

1 regular wrap

2–3 slices of cooked roast beef

¼ green pepper, cored, deseeded and finely sliced

a few slices of red onion

a few slices of provolone cheese

Lay the wrap on a chopping board and cut a slit from the centre to the bottom edge.

In your mind, divide the wrap into quarters. Working clockwise, place the beef on the bottom left quarter, the green pepper on the next quarter, the onion on the third and the provolone on the fourth.

Fold your wrap.

Place the wrap on a hot griddle pan and cook for 2 minutes. Flip and cook on the other side for a further 2 minutes until the beef is piping hot and the wrap is golden and toasted. Serve immediately.

LEFTOVER ROAST

1 regular wrap

100g (3½oz) leftover roast meat, such as chicken, beef, pork or lamb, or vegetarian nut roast, chopped

2 roast potatoes, broken up

2 tablespoons suitable sauce, such as mustard, mint sauce, apple sauce or horseradish

50g (1¾oz) leftover cooked vegetables, such as carrots or parsnips, mashed

hot gravy, for dipping

Lay the wrap on a chopping board and cut a slit from the centre to the bottom edge.

In your mind, divide the wrap into quarters. Working clockwise, place the meat or nut roast on the bottom left quarter and the roast potatoes on the next quarter, spread the sauce over the third and place the vegetables on the fourth.

Fold your wrap.

Place the wrap on a hot griddle pan and cook for 2 minutes. Flip and cook on the other side for a further 2 minutes until the fillings are piping hot and the wrap is golden and toasted. Serve immediately with gravy for dipping.

FISH FINGER SANDWICH

1 regular wrap

3–4 fish fingers, freshly cooked

1 tablespoon tartare sauce

juice of ¼ lemon

small handful of shredded Little Gem lettuce or Romaine heart

50g (1¾oz) frozen peas, freshly cooked

Lay the wrap on a chopping board and cut a slit from the centre to the bottom edge.

In your mind, divide the wrap into quarters. Working clockwise, place the fish fingers on the bottom left quarter, spread the tartare sauce over the next quarter and place the lettuce on the third and the peas on the fourth.

Fold your wrap.

Place the wrap on a hot griddle pan and cook for 2 minutes. Flip and cook on the other side for a further 2 minutes until golden and toasted. Serve immediately.

SHREDDED PORK

1 regular wrap

100g (3½oz) ready-prepared pulled pork, freshly cooked and shredded

½ avocado, sliced

4 tablespoons canned refried beans, heated

50g (1¾oz) Monterey Jack cheese, grated

Lay the wrap on a chopping board and cut a slit from the centre to the bottom edge.

In your mind, divide the wrap into quarters. Working clockwise, place the pork on the bottom left quarter, the avocado on the next quarter, the refried beans on the third and the Monterey Jack on the fourth.

Fold your wrap.

Place the wrap on a hot griddle pan and cook for 2 minutes. Flip and cook on the other side for a further 2 minutes until the fillings are piping hot and the wrap is golden and toasted. Serve immediately.

FALAFEL

1 regular wrap

2 tablespoons hummus

3–4 falafel, freshly cooked and broken up

small handful of shredded Iceberg lettuce

1 tomato, sliced

small handful of pickled turnips, chopped if large

Lay the wrap on a chopping board and cut a slit from the centre to the bottom edge.

In your mind, divide the wrap into quarters. Working clockwise, spread the hummus over the bottom left quarter, then place the falafel on the next quarter, the lettuce and tomato on the third and the pickled turnips on the fourth.

Fold your wrap, then serve.

CHILLI DOG

1 regular wrap

1 large hot dog sausage, freshly cooked and sliced

a few slices of red onion

1 teaspoon sliced green jalapeños from a jar

1 teaspoon mild yellow mustard

75g (2¾oz) ready-prepared chilli con carne, heated

Lay the wrap on a chopping board and cut a slit from the centre to the bottom edge.

In your mind, divide the wrap into quarters. Working clockwise, place the sausage on the bottom left quarter, the onion and jalapeños on the next quarter, spread the mustard over the third and place the chilli on the fourth.

Fold your wrap.

Place the wrap on a hot griddle pan and cook for 2 minutes. Flip and cook on the other side for a further 2 minutes until the fillings are piping hot and the wrap is golden and toasted. Serve immediately.

ALTERNATIVES

Polish: swap the hot dog sausage for smoked chicken sausage and the chilli for sauerkraut.

Vegan: swap the chilli for spicy refried beans and use a vegan hot dog sausage.

Chipotle Cheese: swap the jalapeños for a sprinkling of mature Cheddar cheese and the mustard for chipotle mayonnaise.

STEAK & KIMCHI

1 regular wrap

5–6 slices of freshly cooked steak

1 tablespoon mayonnaise

1 teaspoon sriracha

30g (1oz) kimchi

1 spring onion, sliced

a chunk of cucumber, cut into matchsticks

Lay the wrap on a chopping board and cut a slit from the centre to the bottom edge.

In your mind, divide the wrap into quarters. Working clockwise, place the steak on the bottom left quarter, spread the mayonnaise and sriracha over the next quarter, place the kimchi on the third and the spring onion and cucumber on the fourth.

Fold your wrap, then serve.

Alternatively, place the wrap on a hot griddle pan and cook for 2 minutes. Flip and cook on the other side for a further 2 minutes until golden and toasted. Serve immediately.

CURRIED HUMMUS

1 regular wrap

1 tablespoon vegan curry sauce

2 tablespoons hummus

small handful of spinach

2 tablespoons mango chutney

¼ red pepper, sliced

Lay the wrap on a chopping board and cut a slit from the centre to the bottom edge.

In your mind, divide the wrap into quarters. Working clockwise, spread the curry sauce and hummus over the bottom left quarter, place the spinach on the next quarter, spread the mango chutney over the third and place the pepper on the fourth.

Fold your wrap.

Place the wrap on a hot griddle pan and cook for 2 minutes. Flip and cook on the other side for a further 2 minutes until golden and toasted. Serve immediately.

PARMIGIANA

1 regular wrap

5-6 slices of roasted aubergine from a jar

2 tablespoons tomato sauce

½ mozzarella cheese ball, about 60g (2¼oz), shredded

1 tablespoon vegetarian basil pesto

Lay the wrap on a chopping board and cut a slit from the centre to the bottom edge.

In your mind, divide the wrap into quarters. Working clockwise, place the aubergine on the bottom left quarter, spread the tomato sauce over the next quarter, place the mozzarella on the third and spread the pesto over the fourth.

Fold your wrap.

Place the wrap on a hot griddle pan and cook for 2 minutes. Flip and cook on the other side for a further 2 minutes until golden and toasted. Serve immediately.

CHIPOTLE & BLACK BEAN

1 regular wrap

1 teaspoon vegan chipotle sauce

100g (3½oz) drained canned black beans, heated and mashed

½ avocado, sliced

2 tablespoons tomato salsa

Lay the wrap on a chopping board and cut a slit from the centre to the bottom edge.

In your mind, divide the wrap into quarters. Working clockwise, spread the chipotle sauce over the bottom left quarter, then place the beans on the next quarter, the avocado on the third and the salsa on the fourth.

Fold your wrap.

Place the wrap on a hot griddle pan and cook for 2 minutes. Flip and cook on the other side for a further 2 minutes until golden and toasted. Serve immediately.

ALTERNATIVES

Cheese: swap the avocado for slices of Red Leicester cheese.

Chilli: swap the chipotle sauce for crushed tortilla chips and the black beans for bean chilli con carne.

Meat: swap the beans for chilli con carne.

SALAMI & GRUYÈRE

1 regular wrap

5–6 slices of salami

50g (1¾oz) Gruyère cheese, grated

1 large gherkin, sliced

1 tablespoon mayonnaise

1 teaspoon Dijon mustard

Lay the wrap on a chopping board and cut a slit from the centre to the bottom edge.

In your mind, divide the wrap into quarters. Working clockwise, place the salami on the bottom left quarter, the Gruyère on the next quarter and the gherkin on the third, then spread the mayonnaise and mustard over the fourth.

Fold your wrap, then serve.

FAJITA

1 regular wrap

2 tablespoons tomato salsa

5-6 coriander leaves

½ avocado, sliced

100g (3½oz) shredded cooked chicken

1 roasted red pepper from a jar, sliced

Lay the wrap on a chopping board and cut a slit from the centre to the bottom edge.

In your mind, divide the wrap into quarters. Working clockwise, place the salsa and coriander leaves on the bottom left quarter, the avocado on the next quarter, the chicken on the third and the pepper on the fourth.

Fold your wrap.

Place the wrap on a hot griddle pan and cook for 2 minutes. Flip and cook on the other side for a further 2 minutes until the chicken is piping hot and the wrap is golden and toasted. Serve immediately.

FISH TACO

1 regular wrap

4 fish goujons, freshly cooked

small handful of shredded red cabbage

½ avocado, mashed

juice of ¼ lime

2 tablespoons tomato salsa

Lay the wrap on a chopping board and cut a slit from the centre to the bottom edge.

In your mind, divide the wrap into quarters. Working clockwise, place the fish goujons on the bottom left quarter and the red cabbage on the next quarter. Place the avocado on the third quarter and squeeze over the lime juice, then place the tomato salsa on the fourth.

Fold your wrap, then serve.

LAMB KOFTA

1 regular wrap

2 lamb koftas or kebabs, freshly cooked and broken up

1 tablespoon tzatziki

pinch of sumac

1 tablespoon hummus

small handful of mixed salad leaves

a few slices of red onion

Lay the wrap on a chopping board and cut a slit from the centre to the bottom edge.

In your mind, divide the wrap into quarters. Working clockwise, place the koftas or kebabs on the bottom left quarter, then spread the tzatziki over the next quarter and sprinkle with the sumac. Spread the hummus over the third quarter and place the salad leaves and onion on the fourth.

Fold your wrap, then serve.

PLOUGHMAN'S

1 regular wrap

50g (1¾oz) vegetarian mature Cheddar cheese, sliced

1 tablespoon chutney – use your favourite

small handful of salad leaves

½ apple, cored and sliced

Lay the wrap on a chopping board and cut a slit from the centre to the bottom edge.

In your mind, divide the wrap into quarters. Working clockwise, place the Cheddar on the bottom left quarter, spread the chutney over the next quarter and place the salad leaves on the third and the apple on the fourth.

Fold your wrap, then serve.

ALTERNATIVES

Meat: swap the cheese for sliced ham or sliced pork pie.

Vegan: swap the Cheddar cheese for vegan cream cheese.

Pickled: swap the chutney for quick-pickled red onions.

KETCHUP & FRIES

1 regular wrap

200g (7oz) French fries, freshly cooked

1 tablespoon mayonnaise

1 tablespoon tomato ketchup

Lay the wrap on a chopping board and cut a slit from the centre to the bottom edge.

In your mind, divide the wrap into quarters. Working clockwise, place half the fries on the bottom left quarter, spread the mayonnaise over the next quarter, place the remaining fries on the third and spread the ketchup over the fourth.

Fold your wrap.

Place the wrap on a hot griddle pan and cook for 2 minutes. Flip and cook on the other side for a further 2 minutes until golden and toasted. Serve immediately.

CAPRESE

1 regular wrap

small handful of spinach

1 tomato, sliced

4 basil leaves

½ mozzarella cheese ball, about 60g (2½oz), shredded

1 tablespoon vegetarian basil pesto

Lay the wrap on a chopping board and cut a slit from the centre to the bottom edge.

In your mind, divide the wrap into quarters. Working clockwise, place the spinach on the bottom left quarter and the tomato on the next quarter, topped with the basil. Place the mozzarella on the third, then spread the pesto over the fourth.

Fold your wrap, then serve.

Alternatively, place the wrap on a hot griddle pan and cook for 2 minutes. Flip and cook on the other side for a further 2 minutes until golden and toasted. Serve immediately.

SOMETHING SWEET

BANANA, CARAMEL & CHOCOLATE

1 regular wrap

½ banana, sliced

2 caramelized biscuits, crumbled

1 tablespoon hazelnut and chocolate spread

1 tablespoon dulce de leche

Lay the wrap on a chopping board and cut a slit from the centre to the bottom edge.

In your mind, divide the wrap into quarters. Working clockwise, place the banana on the bottom left quarter and sprinkle the biscuit crumbs over the next quarter, then cover the third with the hazelnut and chocolate spread and the fourth with the dulce de leche.

Fold your wrap.

Place the wrap on a hot griddle pan and cook for 2 minutes. Flip and cook on the other side for a further 2 minutes until golden and toasted. Serve immediately.

BLUEBERRY & ALMOND

1 regular wrap

1 tablespoon blueberry jam

2 tablespoons vegan cream cheese

50g (1¾oz) blueberries, roughly mashed

1 tablespoon almond butter

Lay the wrap on a chopping board and cut a slit from the centre to the bottom edge.

In your mind, divide the wrap into quarters. Working clockwise, spread the jam over the bottom left quarter and the cream cheese over the next quarter, then place the blueberries on the third and spread the almond butter over the fourth.

Fold your wrap, then serve.

ALTERNATIVES

Raspberry: swap the blueberry jam for raspberry jam and the blueberries for raspberries.

Blueberry Crumble: sprinkle one crumbled shortbread biscuit and a pinch of ground cinnamon over the cream cheese.

Tropical: swap the blueberries for sliced pineapple or papaya and sprinkle with grated lime zest.

ETON MESS

1 regular wrap

a few strawberries, sliced

spray whipped cream

2-3 mini meringues, broken up

1 tablespoon strawberry jam

Lay the wrap on a chopping board and cut a slit from the centre to the bottom edge.

In your mind, divide the wrap into quarters. Working clockwise, place the strawberries on the bottom left quarter, squirt the cream over the next quarter, sprinkle the meringues over the third and spread the jam over the fourth.

Fold your wrap, then serve.

ALTERNATIVES

Mixed Berry: swap the strawberries for mixed berries and the strawberry jam for cherry jam.

Sweet and Sour: swap the meringues for chocolate chips and the jam for lemon curd.

Tropical: swap the strawberries for mango and the strawberry jam for passionfruit jam.

PBJ

1 regular wrap

2 tablespoons smooth peanut butter

½ banana, sliced

2 tablespoons strawberry jam

2 tablespoons chocolate spread

Lay the wrap on a chopping board and cut a slit from the centre to the bottom edge.

In your mind, divide the wrap into quarters. Working clockwise, spread the peanut butter over the bottom left quarter, place the banana slices on the next quarter, spread the jam over the third and the chocolate spread over the fourth.

Fold your wrap, then serve.

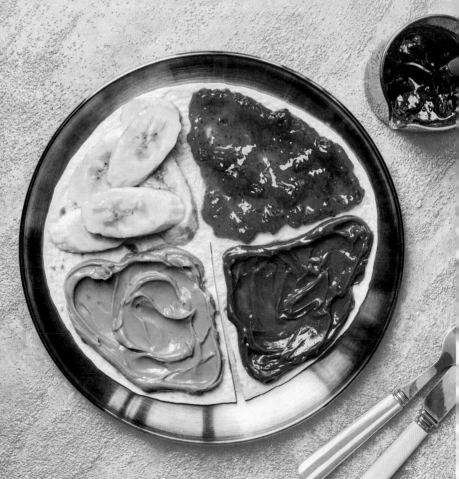

CHOCOLATE ORANGE ❄ ✓

1 regular wrap

2 tablespoons bitter orange marmalade

4 tablespoons hazelnut and chocolate spread

6–7 orange segments

Lay the wrap on a chopping board and cut a slit from the centre to the bottom edge.

In your mind, divide the wrap into quarters. Working clockwise, spread the marmalade over the bottom left quarter and half the hazelnut and chocolate spread over the next quarter. Place the orange segments on the third and the remaining spread over the fourth.

Fold your wrap, then serve.

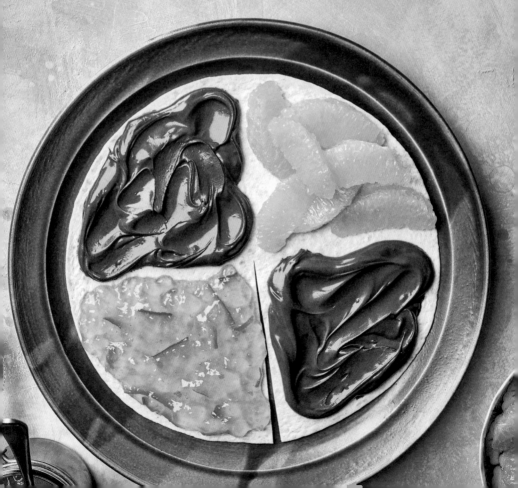

S'MORES

2 tablespoons hazelnut
and chocolate spread

2 tablespoons
marshmallow spread

2 digestive biscuits,
crumbled

½ banana, sliced

Lay the wrap on a chopping board and cut a slit from the centre to the bottom edge.

In your mind, divide the wrap into quarters. Working clockwise, cover the bottom left quarter with the hazelnut and chocolate spread and the next quarter with the marshmallow spread, then sprinkle the biscuit crumbs over the third and place the banana on the fourth.

Fold your wrap.

Place the wrap on a hot griddle pan and cook for 2 minutes. Flip and cook on the other side for a further 2 minutes until golden and toasted. Serve immediately.

BLACK FOREST

1 regular wrap

2 tablespoons cherry jam

2 tablespoons Greek yogurt

2 tablespoons hazelnut and chocolate spread

small handful of crumbled chocolate sponge

Lay the wrap on a chopping board and cut a slit from the centre to the bottom edge.

In your mind, divide the wrap into quarters. Working clockwise, spread the jam over the bottom left quarter, the yogurt over the next quarter and the hazelnut and chocolate spread over the third, then sprinkle the chocolate sponge over the fourth.

Fold your wrap, then serve.

APRICOT & RASPBERRY

1 regular wrap

2 tablespoons apricot compote or apricot spread

2 tablespoons vegan cream cheese

1 tablespoon roughly chopped roasted pistachios

1 fresh apricot or 2 canned apricot halves, sliced

6–8 raspberries, roughly mashed

Lay the wrap on a chopping board and cut a slit from the centre to the bottom edge.

In your mind, divide the wrap into quarters. Working clockwise, spread the compote over the bottom left quarter, then the cream cheese over the next quarter and sprinkle the pistachios on top. Place the apricot on the third quarter and the raspberries on the fourth.

Fold your wrap, then serve.

APPLE & BLACKBERRY CRUMBLE

1 regular wrap

1 tablespoon blackberry jam

½ apple, cored and sliced

2 tablespoons Greek yogurt

2 shortbread biscuits, crumbled

hot custard, for dipping

Lay the wrap on a chopping board and cut a slit from the centre to the bottom edge.

In your mind, divide the wrap into quarters. Working clockwise, spread the jam over the bottom left quarter, place the apple on the next quarter, spread the yogurt over the third and sprinkle the shortbread crumbs over the fourth.

Fold your wrap.

Place the wrap on a hot griddle pan and cook for 2 minutes. Flip and cook on the other side for a further 2 minutes until golden and toasted. Serve immediately with custard for dipping.

RHUBARB & CUSTARD

1 regular wrap

2 tablespoons rhubarb compote

2 tablespoons custard

a few strawberries, sliced

6–8 raspberries, roughly mashed

Lay the wrap on a chopping board and cut a slit from the centre to the bottom edge.

In your mind, divide the wrap into quarters. Working clockwise, spread the compote over the bottom left quarter and the custard over the next quarter, then place the strawberries on the third and the raspberries on the fourth.

Fold your wrap.

Place the wrap on a hot griddle pan and cook for 2 minutes. Flip and cook on the other side for a further 2 minutes until golden and toasted. Serve immediately.

CHARRED PINEAPPLE & MANGO 🔥❄✔

1 regular wrap

6 fresh pineapple fingers

2 tablespoons mango purée or puréed fresh mango

2 tablespoons mascarpone cheese

finely grated zest of ½ lime

Lay the wrap on a chopping board and cut a slit from the centre to the bottom edge.

Using a kitchen blowtorch or very hot grill, scorch or grill the pineapple fingers briefly until golden and a little charred.

In your mind, divide the wrap into quarters. Working clockwise, spread the mango purée over the bottom left quarter and place half the pineapple on the next quarter. Spread the mascarpone over the third quarter and sprinkle with the lime zest, then place the remaining pineapple on the fourth.

Fold your wrap, then serve.

Alternatively, place the wrap on a hot griddle pan and cook for 2 minutes. Flip and cook on the other side for a further 2 minutes until golden and toasted. Serve immediately.

FIG & HONEY

1 regular wrap

5–6 slices of fig

2 tablespoons ricotta cheese

½ teaspoon sesame seeds

2 tablespoons honey

1 tablespoon almond butter

Lay the wrap on a chopping board and cut a slit from the centre to the bottom edge.

In your mind, divide the wrap into quarters. Working clockwise, place the fig on the bottom left quarter, then spread the ricotta over the next quarter and sprinkle with the sesame seeds. Spread the honey over the third quarter and the almond butter over the fourth.

Fold your wrap, then serve.

Alternatively, place the wrap on a hot griddle pan and cook for 2 minutes. Flip and cook on the other side for a further 2 minutes until golden and toasted. Serve immediately.

PEAR & CHOCOLATE

1 regular wrap

2–3 canned pear halves, sliced

2 tablespoons hazelnut and chocolate spread

1 tablespoon almond butter

Lay the wrap on a chopping board and cut a slit from the centre to the bottom edge.

In your mind, divide the wrap into quarters. Working clockwise, place half the pear slices on the bottom left quarter and cover the next quarter with the hazelnut and chocolate spread, then place the remaining pear slices on the third and spread the almond butter over the fourth.

Fold your wrap, then serve.

PEACH & CINNAMON

1 regular wrap

5–6 slices of peach

½ teaspoon ground cinnamon

2 tablespoons blueberry jam

2 tablespoons ricotta cheese

1 tablespoon toasted coconut chips

Lay the wrap on a chopping board and cut a slit from the centre to the bottom edge.

In your mind, divide the wrap into quarters. Working clockwise, place half the peach slices on the bottom left quarter, sprinkled with half the cinnamon. Spread the jam over the next quarter. Place the remaining peach slices on the third, sprinkled with the remaining cinnamon. Spread the ricotta over the fourth quarter and sprinkle with the coconut.

Fold your wrap, then serve.

INDEX

GLOSSARY

UK   US

aubergine / eggplant

bacon rasher / bacon slice

beetroot / beet

biscuits / cookies

celeriac / celery root

chicken goujons / crispy chicken strips
or tenders

chopping board / cutting board

coriander / cilantro

courgette / zucchini

crisps / potato chips

digestive biscuits / Graham crackers

dill / dill weed

fish fingers / fish sticks

fish goujons / crispy fish strips
or tenders

frying pan / skillet

full-fat natural yogurt / whole milk
plain yogurt

griddle pan / grill pan

grill / broiler (n.); broil (v.)

hard-boiled egg / hard-cooked egg

mature Cheddar cheese / sharp
Cheddar cheese

nonstick baking paper / nonstick
parchment paper

packet instructions / package
directions

pepper, red or green / bell pepper,
red or green

prawn crackers / shrimp chips

prawns / shrimp

rocket / arugula

salad leaves / salad greens

soured cream / sour cream

spring onion / scallion

wholemeal / whole wheat

First published in Great Britain
in 2021 by Hamlyn, an imprint of
Octopus Publishing Group Ltd
Carmelite House
50 Victoria Embankment
London EC4Y 0DZ
www.octopusbooks.co.uk

An Hachette UK Company
www.hachette.co.uk

Copyright © Octopus Publishing Group
Limited 2021

Distributed in the US by
Hachette Book Group
1290 Avenue of the Americas
4th and 5th Floors
New York, NY 10104

Distributed in Canada by
Canadian Manda Group
664 Annette St.
Toronto, Ontario, Canada M6S 2C8

Natalie Thomson asserts the moral
right to be identified as the author
of this work.

ISBN 978-0-600-63726-4

A CIP catalogue record for this book
is available from the British Library.

Printed and bound in China

10 9 8 7 6 5 4 3 2 1

Publishing Director: Eleanor Maxfield
Editor: Ella Parsons
Copyeditor: Jo Richardson
Deputy Art Director: Jaz Bahra
Photographer: Charlotte Nott-Macaire
Props stylist: Agathe Gits
Food stylist: Felicity Price-Thomas
Senior Production Controller: Allison
   Gonsalves

Standard level spoon measurement are
used in all recipes.
1 tablespoon = one 15ml spoon
1 teaspoon = one 5ml spoon

Both imperial and metric measurements
have been given in all recipes. Use one
set of measurements only and not a
mixture of both.